Landscape Touch
Vol. 1

Sun Mi Kwon

Copyright © 2024 Sun Mi Kwon

Illustrations Copyright © 2024 Sun Mi Kwon

All rights reserved.

ISBN: 978-1-963967-08-1

No portion of this book may be reproduced in any form without written permission from the author, except as permitted by U.S. copyright law.

Visit us at www.landscapetouch.com

ABOUT THIS BOOK

Welcome to a visual journey designed to inspire outdoor living possibilities. This book is crafted with the vision of empowering new homeowners to curate outdoor spaces that resonate with their lifestyle, while offering contractors and architects fresh perspectives and innovative ideas to elevate their craft, portfolios, and businesses. It serves as a valuable educational resource for students striving for excellence in their projects. With stunning and distinctive night views illuminated by captivating lighting designs, this book stands out as a unique treasure in its genre. Join us now as we explore the realm of endless possibilities. May this book guide you towards achieving your desired outdoor oasis. Whether you choose to implement the entire design or incorporate select elements, you'll find endless inspiration to enhance your outdoor living experience.

TABLE OF CONTENTS

House 1 - Day View

1	**2D HOUSE FLOOR PLAN**
2 - 12	**3D HOUSE & DAY ISO VIEW**
13	**HOUSE FRONT & SIDE YARD VIEW** R.V. camp parking & backyard
14 - 20	**BACKYARD VIEW 1** Twin patio cover lounge, open lounge w/fire pit & BBQ dining area
21 - 28	**BACKYARD VIEW 2** Pool cabana w/fire pit lounge, cantilever bench, open patio cover over the pool, outdoor shower, pool deck lounge w/open patio cover
29 - 32	**BACKYARD VIEW 3** Raised deck w/solid cover patio, lower deck floor lounge w/fire pit & private shade lounge
33 - 39	**BACKYARD VIEW 4** Pool, Spa/Foot Spa, Pool & Spa lounge & Home camp ground

House 1 - Night View

40	**2D HOUSE FLOOR PLAN**
41 - 51	**3D HOUSE & NIGHT ISO VIEW**
52 - 53	**HOUSE FRONT & SIDE YARD VIEW** House front entry, front landscape, side yard, R.V. camp parking & open lounge
54 - 60	**BACKYARD VIEW 1** Twin open patio cover lounge w/interior layout, open lounge w/fire pit, BBQ w/dining, pool deck lounge w/safety rail
61 - 73	**BACKYARD VIEW 2** Pool cabana w/fire pit lounge, seating bench w/accent fire pit at raised deck entry access, outdoor shower w/vanity/bath layout options, pool & pool cover patio

Day View

2D FLOOR PLAN VIEW

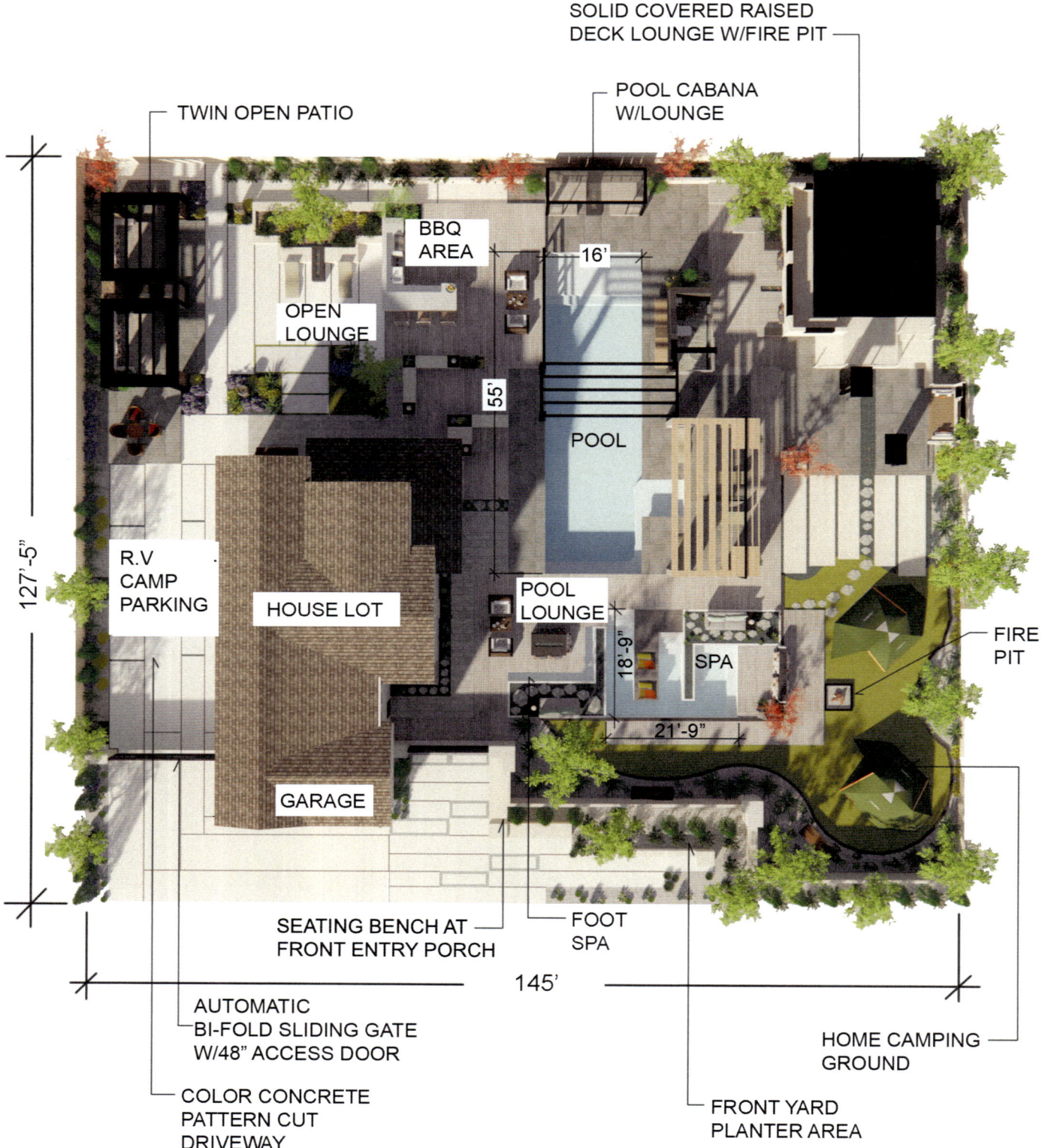

3D HOUSE VIEW 1

3D HOUSE VIEW 2

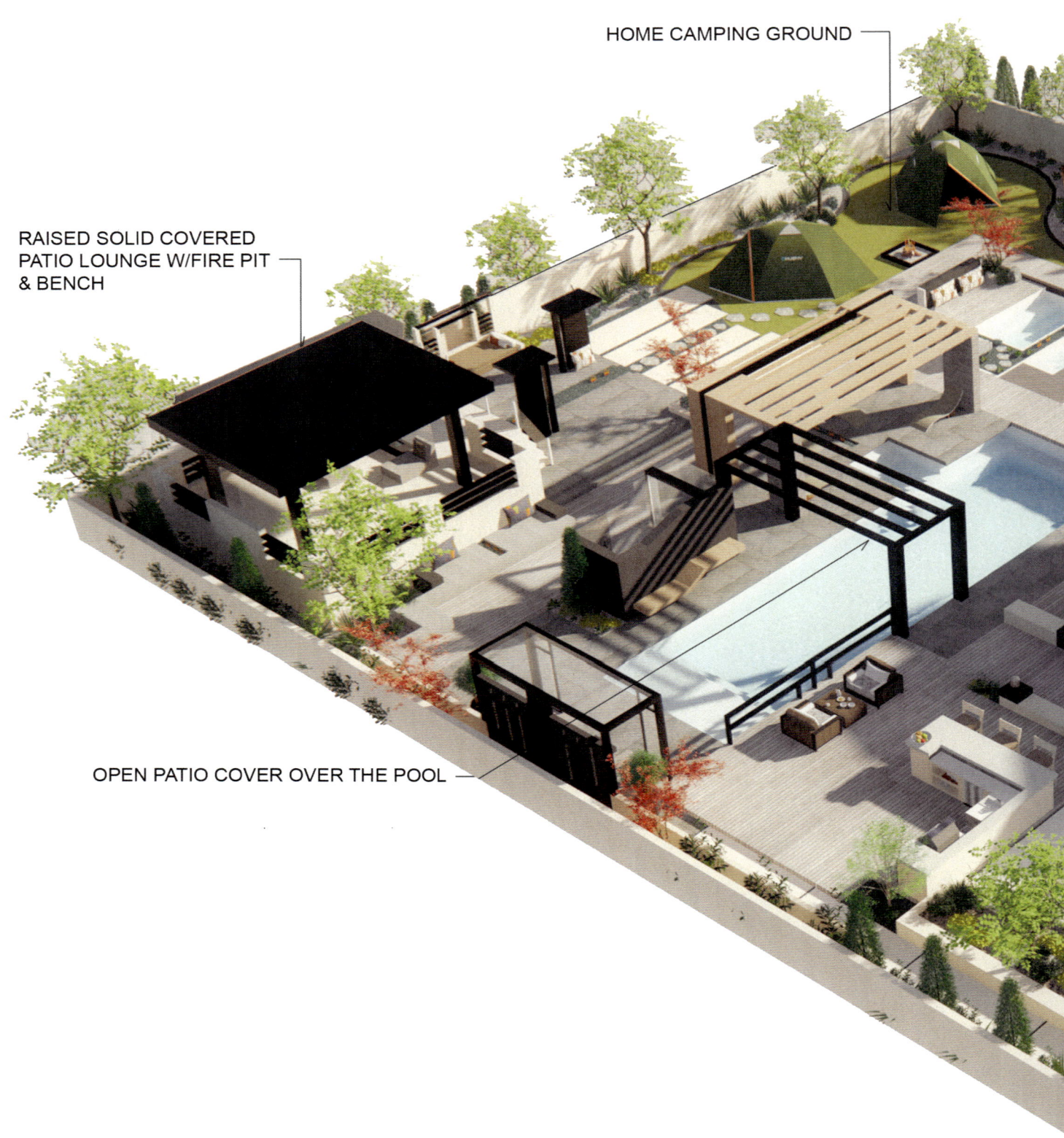

HOME CAMPING GROUND

RAISED SOLID COVERED PATIO LOUNGE W/FIRE PIT & BENCH

OPEN PATIO COVER OVER THE POOL

PG 4

3D HOUSE VIEW 3

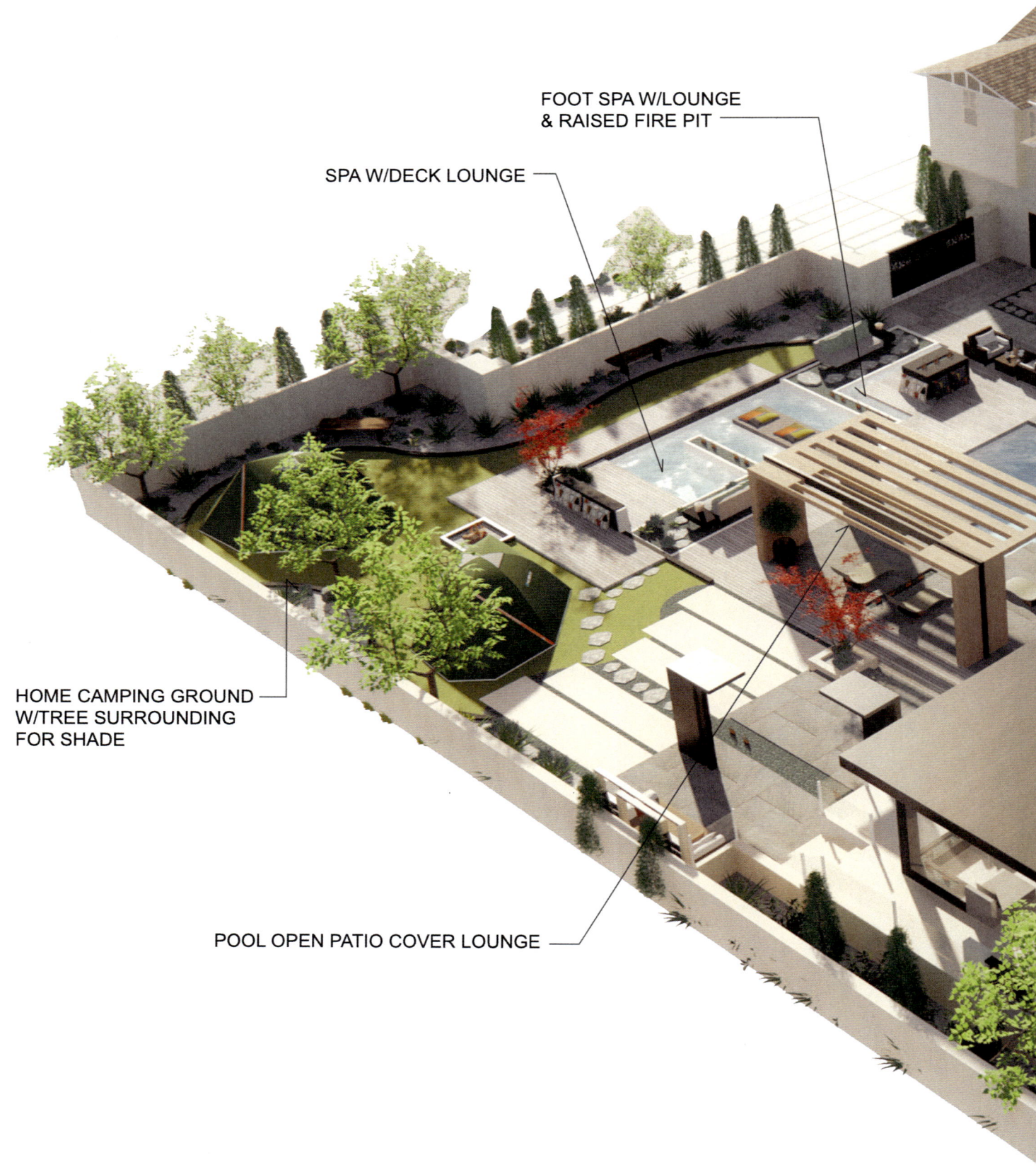

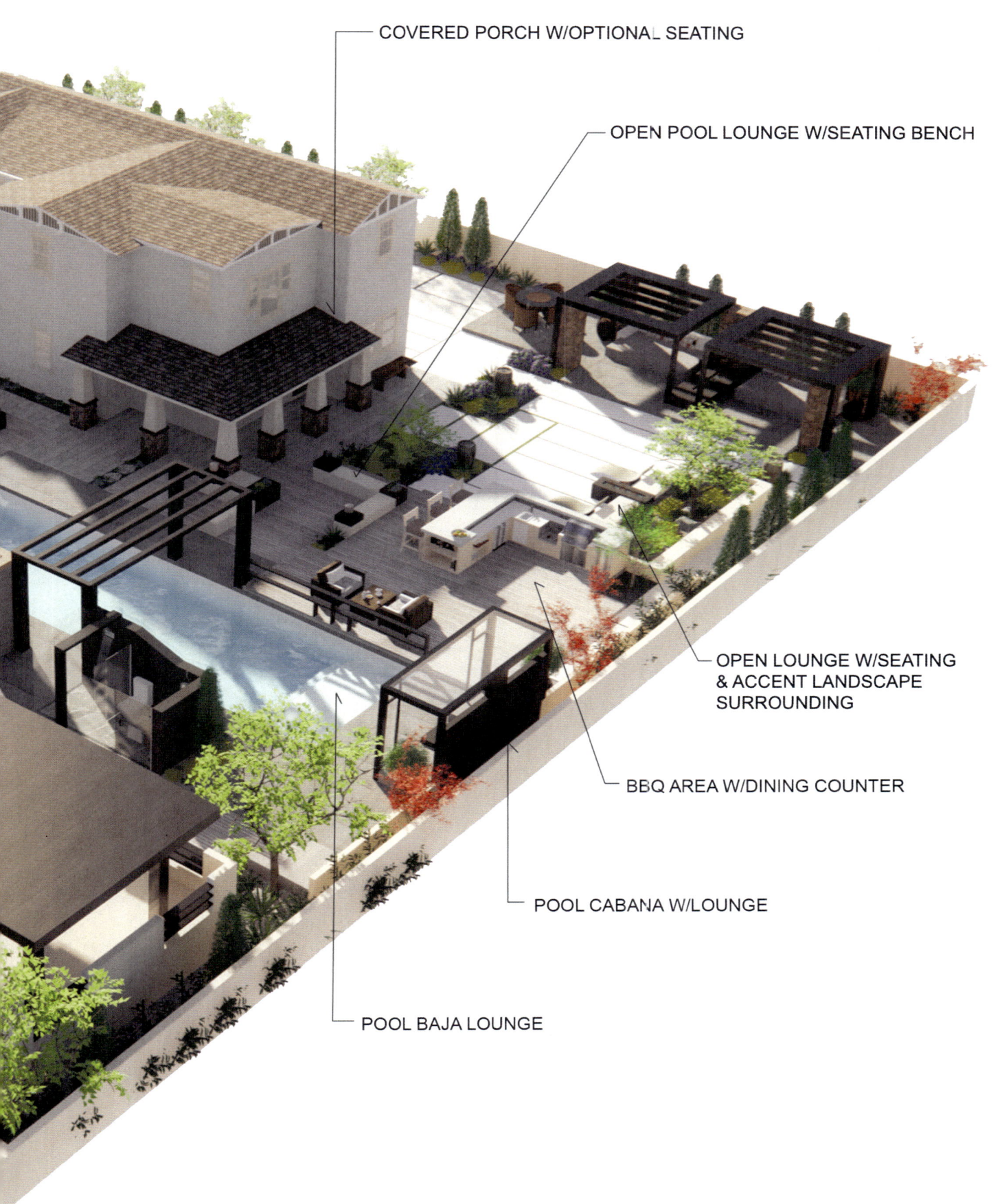

HOUSE FRONT ISO VIEW

HOUSE RIGHT ISO VIEW

HOUSE LEFT ISO VIEW

OPEN PATIO LOUNGE

COLOR CONCRETE W/DECORATIVE
PATTERN CUT R.V. CAMP PARKING

AUTOMATIC BI-FOLD SLIDING GATE W/48" ACCESS DOOR

TWIN OPEN PATIO COVER LOUNGE W/DAYBED & FIRE PIT

1 STEP UP

TWIN OPEN PATIO LOUNGE INTERIOR VIEW

ACCENT POTTED PLANTS

SMOOTH STUCCO BACKING & ARMREST

PORCELAIN TILE SEATING

TWIN OPEN PATIO LOUNGE W/ BENCH & FIRE PIT

OPEN LOUNGE W/LANDSCAPE SURROUNDING

OPEN LOUNGE
SEATING AREA
W/FIRE PIT

ACCENT WATER FEATURE
OR BIRD BATH

BBQ LAYOUT

PG 20

MANUFACTURED SLAB STONE COUNTER TOP

ACCENT MOSAIC TILE

WOOD PLANK LOOK PORCELAIN TILE FLOORING

SMOOTH STUCCO VENEER

OPEN POOL LOUNGE
W/SEATING BENCH

BBQ DINING
&
POOL COPING LOUNGE AREA

POWDER COATED
42"HT SAFETY RAIL

POOL CABANA W/FIRE PIT BENCH LOUNGE VIEW

ACCENT CANTILEVER BENCH BEHIND SHOWER WALL

PORCELAIN TILE FINISH SEATING BENCH W/ACCENT FIRE PIT

OPEN PATIO COVER OVER THE POOL

OUTDOOR SHOWER W/FULL SHOWER OPTION

NATURAL STONE FLOORING
OVERSIZE PORCELAIN TILED WALLS

SOLID COVER ROOFING
RECOMMENDED FOR
FULL SHOWER OPTION

SHOWER

BENCH &
FIRE PIT

POOL

CABANA LOUNGE

OPEN PATIO COVER LOUNGE BY THE POOL

POOL ENTRY VIEW W/OPEN PATIO COVER

RAISED COVER PATIO LOUNGE ENTRY STEP ACCESS

LOWER DECK LOUNGE W/FLOOR FIRE PIT
AT COVERED FLOOR SEATING

UPPER DECK STEP ACCESS

LOWER DECK LOUNGE PORTABLE DAYBED FLOOR LOUNGE VIEW

SOLID COVER RAISED DECK LOUNGE W/SEATING BENCH & FIRE PIT

HOME CAMPING GROUND W/POOL VIEW

HOME CAMPING GROUND & SPA VIEW

CAMPING GROUND W/SPA & RAISED DECK AREA VIEW

POOL & SPA AREA OVER VIEW

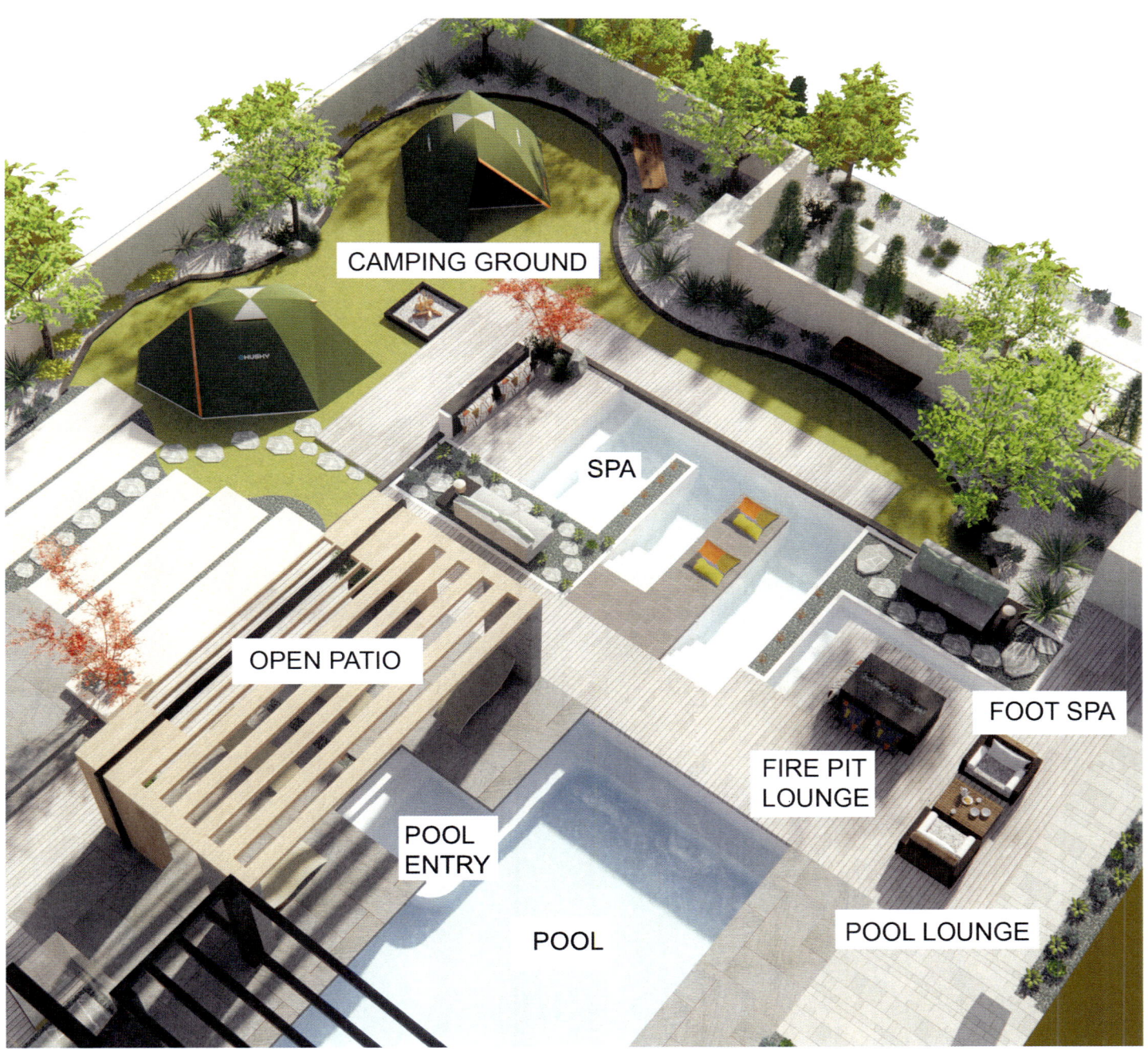

POOL LOUNGE VIEW W/FOOT SPA & FIRE PIT

OPEN PATIO COVER OVER THE POOL

Night View

2D FLOOR PLAN VIEW

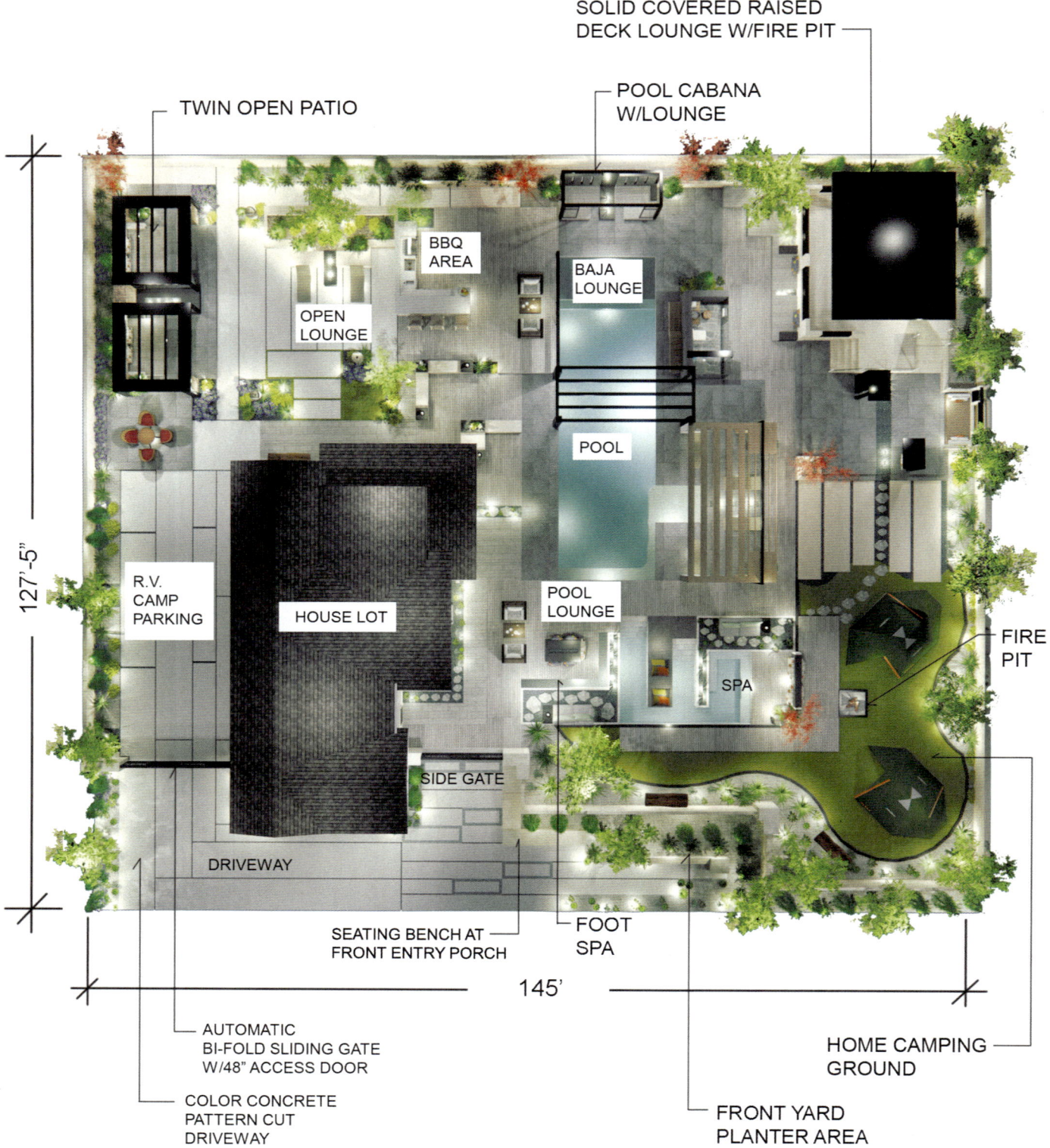

3D HOUSE NIGHT VIEW 1

3D HOUSE NIGHT VIEW 2

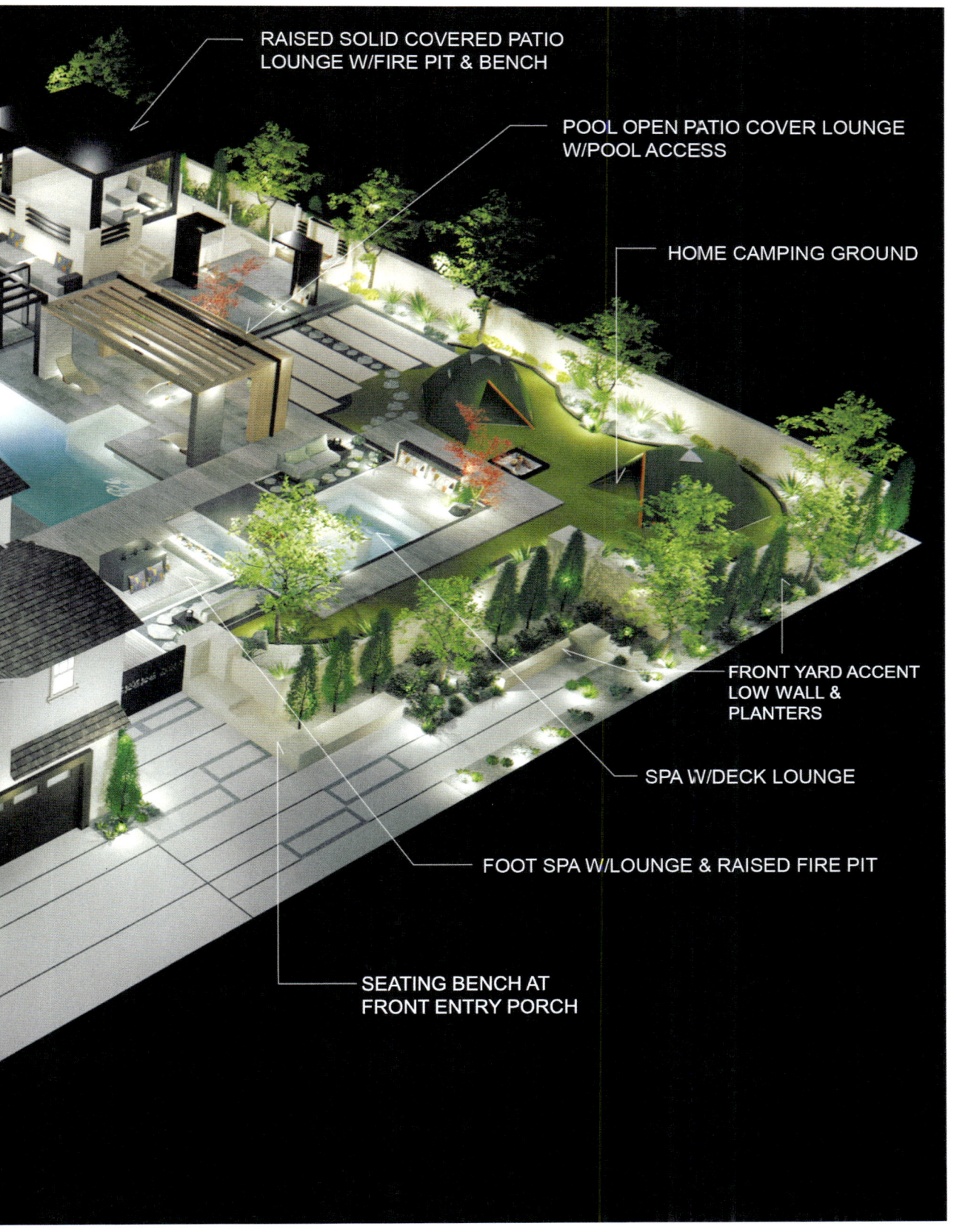

3D HOUSE NIGHT VIEW 3

HOUSE FRONT ISO NIGHT VIEW

HOUSE RIGHT ISO NIGHT VIEW

HOUSE LEFT ISO NIGHT VIEW

RIGHT SIDE OF THE HOUSE OVERALL VIEW

DECORATIVE FIXED IRON FENCE W/5' ENTRY ACCESS DOOR

LEFT SIDE OF THE HOUSE OVERALL VIEW

R.V CAMP PARKING OVER VIEW

OPEN PATIO LOUNGE

TWIN OPEN PATIO & LOUNGE VIEW

BEAUTIFUL NIGHT LOUNGE AREA UNDER THE PATIO...

SOOTHING FIRE PIT... UNDER THE OPEN PATIO COVER

ACCENT WATER FEATURE
OR
BIRD BATH

BBQ AREA WITH OPEN LOUNGE VIEW

BBQ & LOUNGE AREA OVERVIEW

BBQ & DINING AREA OVERVIEW

POOL COPING LOUNGE W/ PATIO FURNITURE SET

POOL CABANA W/TWIN DAYBED & FIRE PIT

PG 61

STUNNING POOL CABANA & LOUNGE VIEW

SEATING BENCH W/FIRE PIT AT RAISED DECK LOUNGE ENTRY

OUTDOOR SHOWER SOLID ROOF COVER IS RECOMMENDED FOR FULL SHOWER (SHOWER, SINK & TOILET)

ACCENT CANTILEVER BENCH BEHIND SHOWER WALL

FIXED IRON OPEN PATIO COVER OVER THE POOL

OPEN PATIO COVER POOL LOUNGE W/FIRE PIT

LOWER DECK LOUNGE VIEW

SEATING BENCH W/FIRE PIT BY RAISED DECK LOUNGE ENTRY

UPPER & LOWER DECK LOUNGE OVERVIEW

LOWER DECK FIRE PIT LOUNGE W/DAYBED

BEAUTIFUL POOL NIGHT VIEW ....

YOUR OWN NIGHT OASIS ...

ABOUT THE AUTHOR

Sun Mi Kwon brings over 23 years of experience as a living space and landscape designer, enriched by extensive hands-on expertise. With a robust background in on-site work, she possesses a deep understanding of practical landscape design principles. Throughout her career, Sun Mi has collaborated with a wide spectrum of clients, including private individuals, industry-independent contractors, and architects. Collectively, her contributions have led to the creation of over 1000 unique designs, showcasing her versatility and innovation in the field.

Made in the USA
Las Vegas, NV
09 January 2025

16124400R00050